The Thinking Revolution
A New Model on Transforming Your Life by Renewing Your Mind

By Myron E. Cobb
with Dr. Foluso Lawal-Solarin

Disclaimer: The material in the book written by Dr. Foluso Lawal-Solarin is not a substitute for counseling, mental health treatment, education, psychological advice, or any other services provided by a psychologist. If you think you may be experiencing any mental health difficulties, or are in need of education, counseling, advice, or other mental health services contact an appropriate mental health counselor or educator. Material written by Dr. Foluso Lawal-Solarin will be designated as such.
Author: Foluso Lawal-Solarin, Ph.D.

The Thinking Revolution
A New Model on Transforming Your Life by Renewing Your Mind

Myron Cobb Copyright © 2015. www.myronecobb.com

All rights reserved. No part of this book may be reproduced or transmitted in any form or by any means, electronic or mechanical, including photocopying, recording, or by any information story or retrieval system, without written permission from the author, except for the inclusion of brief quotations in a review.

Cover Design © 2015 | Christiana Inc | www.cinc-productions.com
Editing | WritersHero, LLC | Atlanta, GA

ISBN: 978-0-692-32653-4

TABLE OF CONTENTS

Acknowledgments V
Forward VII
Introduction IX
1. Thinking...The Missing Ingredient 1
2. Cobb's Renewing Your Mind Model 5
3. Security in Who God made me 7
4. Realization of the Current State of My Life 13
5. Mastering the Mental Toolbox 17
6. Kingdom Thinking 27
7. Fully Transformed Self from a Renewed Mind 39
8. Concluding Thoughts 43

ACKNOWLEDGEMENTS

I would to first thank my Lord Jesus Christ for sending me this assignment.

This book project would not have been possible without the support of many people. The book subject and dynamics matured from numerous discussions and great thinking from Danyelle Jinks-Glenn.

I want to thank Dr. Foluso Lawal-Solarin for her contribution of thinking and writing in the book. My concept and theological readers were Carel Bekker, Melanie Johnson, and Michele Clark Jenkins. Thanks as well to Greg Radcliff for the graphical support.

I also would like to thank Veronica Johnson who moved this project along with her awesome editing skills. She really helped me to finalize the base writing and grammar before sending to final copy editor Lisa Gibson. Getting it over the finish line was Christina Cross and staff.

Thanks to my mother Gloria for all of her years of support and my two beautiful children Harveste and Tyler Cobb.

A special thanks goes out to my lovely wife Tonya Cobb who has pushed me to transform my life during the marriage. She has been my greatest picture of Christ and how to transform one's life through reflection, discipline and hard work.

FORWARD

Every revolution in the history of this world, great or small, started because a person or group decided to think differently about their lives. At the mere thought of living better and being better, individuals were able to forever transform lives. Such is the backdrop of this book that you're about to read – nothing in our lives, for our lives and with our lives will change without us first changing the way we ...And because our lives will never exceed our thinking, Myron Cobb will provide biblical, practical and measurable tools to upgrade our thinking for the purpose of upgrading our lives. This book will unearth beliefs and behaviors that are detrimental for us living confidently as God's child. While at the same time, answering the question of "how to" start changing and staying changed.

The Thinking Revolution is an insightful model of godly and healthy thinking designed to liberate us from accepting a life of self-imposed and circumstance based limitations by helping to cultivate the kind of thinking that brings the fullness of God's presence and power into our everyday life. It's an easy read... great read guaranteed to give a mental model for maximizing our life in... with... for God.

Pastor of Discover Life Church, Speaker, Writer
Roy Barrett
Atlanta, GA

INTRODUCTION

Why I wrote this book

I have always wondered why people do what they do. What is the driving force behind successes and failures? Why do some people beat addictive behaviors and some don't? Why do some people achieve their financial goals and some don't? Why do some people achieve their academic goals and some don't? In my view it goes back to thinking or better yet, transformation.

The scriptural basis of this book is in Romans 12:2 -"Do not conform any longer to the pattern of this world, but be transformed by the renewing of your mind. Then you will be able to test and approve what God's will is – His good, pleasing and perfect will."[1] Many of us have read this Scripture over the years but have never truly understood how a person goes about the process of renewing their mind. Think about a recipe for a dish that has been passed down from generation to generation in your family. There is always that one ingredient that if omitted or incorrectly measured can lead to the dish being less than perfect. Have you ever prepared a dish and had someone taste it and say something is missing? Then, once you pinpointed it, and included that *Missing Ingredient*, the taste of the dish was transformed. That missing ingredient I am referring to is HEALTHY THINKING. I will introduce a new thinking model that will help you achieve the goal of renewing your mind and maintaining its renewed status. Doing this on a daily basis can help you – and others around you.

Critical thinking has been a part of my life for a long time – not just thinking, but analyzing and questioning events that happened in my life, and what I thought about them when they happened. I even have thought years later about how those events shaped my life and those around me.

The one question that comes up each time: Did I have a healthy perspective about that event?

I remember times where I was so adamant about a topic or perspective and realized years later that I was dead wrong. I wonder how my wrong thinking shaped others' lives around me. Did I change someone's outlook for the better or the worse? Some of that wrong thinking was based on an identity crisis. I didn't know who I was because the value I placed on life was "what I had vs. **who's I am.**"

The Thinking Revolution

My parents moved from the city of Chicago to the suburbs the summer before I entered into the seventh grade. We moved from an all-black neighborhood to an all-white neighborhood. I went from being comfortable around who I went to school with and played with to being alienated. It was literally like going to another planet where everyone looks, acts, and speaks differently. There was one kid in the neighborhood who greeted me with kindness, and we became friends for a long time. His family was very nice to me as well, which made the transition a little easier. But I still struggled internally with identity because I was trying to fit in and be liked. I did and said millions of dumb things in the name of popularity. I thought associating with certain people would make other people like me. Well, I was wrong. As I grew older, my thinking was shaped by performance and achievements. No one ever talked to me about just being myself.

I graduated high school in 1986 and attended college at the University of Illinois. Those four years were some of the best years of my life. During my freshman year, I realized that people liked me just for me, so my thinking began to change, and I became less focused on fitting in. My thinking became long-range—doing well in school so that I could have a business career and take care of myself. I began to read many more books about politics, social concepts, business, literature, etc. The question I kept asking myself was, "Who am I in relation to the world and what is my purpose?"

In 1988, I joined Alpha Phi Alpha Fraternity, Inc. This was when I begin to understand the importance of true brotherhood and how what I do and think can affect someone else. One of the concepts taught during the pledging process was to think and act as one team. For example, we all had to memorize the Greek alphabet, then say it out loud. If everyone could not do it, success was not considered. We would all work together until everyone could complete the task. As the saying goes, "No man left behind."

This principle has never left my spirit. God never intended for us to live this life on earth alone. We are connected much more than we sometimes realize. We were designed to think like God and relate to one another deeply. The beauty of it all is that God has been with me the entire time.

As a seventh-grader, I saw my parents run a couple of small businesses. I saw the networking, the business meetings, and the paperwork. That seed was planted early, so as a junior in high school, I took my first accounting course and loved it. After that one class, I knew my path was business and what better way to learn it than to know how to count the money. Now, fast-forward to my junior year in college.

It was around April, and I had an epiphany. I needed a job for the summer AND it had to be related to my major!!! Duhh, I better get working on it. As I started making a few calls, I realized I was on the back end of getting an internship. One day, I told a good friend who mentioned that State Farm in Bloomington, Illinois, has a good program. It was late to submit applications, but I called anyway and got favor to send it, and I did. The program director called me back and said I can have an interview within a week in Bloomington. I immediately called my friend Richard Holloway and said, "I have an interview, and I need some company." Well, the day came, and we got in the car for the hour and fifteen minute ride. We got there early, but as we were waiting we realized I had something on my shirt. Not good, so we quickly found a department store, bought a white oxford shirt, then made it back to the building. I interviewed, and then we drove back to campus. A couple days later, I got the phone call, noting that I had been selected for the program. I believe today that God held that slot for me. I was very happy and excited to get my first real job in Corporate America. That experience with State Farm was absolutely wonderful and helped to solidify that I was to be a marketplace minister – meaning, there was and still is favor given to me by the Lord to influence people for the good in the business world.

That internship was the anchor that allowed me to get a public accounting audit job after I graduated from college. It was that whisper from God – "Get up and get moving" – that started me along my way. There have been these type of experiences and circumstances that have shaped who I am. He knew my tendencies and behaviors and carved a unique path for me to come to Him and receive Christ in my own timing. This decision did not take place until 1996, when I was 28 years old. Since then, I have been on this journey to understand who I am in Jesus Christ.

I got married in 1998 to a lovely Georgia peach named Tonya Smith. I believe I was ready in spirit to get married but not as much in thinking. One of the main drivers of writing this book was a reflection on my thinking in my marriage. I had some wrong thinking that caused my wife Tonya much frustration. I saw the negative effect I had on her, so I had to change or transform, so I could contribute to a healthy Myron, which resulted in a healthier marriage. I am very grateful Tonya kept me around, so I could share with her a better thinking person. Her support has been immeasurable, and I wouldn't be the person I am without her.

In September 2009, I had the privilege of going to Uganda. The purpose of the visit was to minister to the pastors and bishops of Jubilee Christian Life Church under Apostle Wilson and Pastor Priscilla Kulaba. This trip opened my eyes to how people with less than we have in America depend on faith, just as humans depend on water. Needless to say, I was the one who was blessed and the trip changed my thinking regarding faith. The Lord began to speak to me about how to change people's behavior in a healthier and more consistent way. The only way to change behavior is help people change the way they think.

The model that will be presented in this book is grounded in a thinking plan with steps that mirror my ongoing journey to be a healthy thinker in Christ. I write this in the same spirit Peter did in 2 Peter 3:1 "…to stimulate you to wholesome thinking."[1]

That long-standing answer to my question of what drives people's behavior was answered by the Lord in a divine revelation.

In essence, it is who we think we are or who we think we are not that determine our actions and behaviors.

This book is not meant to be a psychological thesis on thinking models with 20 years of research. It is meant to be a view into my life of thinking and how the Lord gave me an opportunity to share a concept on how to transform our lives through the renewing of our minds. The Lord Jesus Christ states in Matthew 10:39, "Whoever finds his life will lose it, and whoever loses his life for my sake will find it."[1] I am urging you to decide to find your life now and then lose it so that Christ can live through you. Be someone that knows who they really are and reflect the light outward that is within.

As we move into the first chapter of the book, let's define thinking. The Merriam-Webster dictionary definition of *THINKING* is the action of using one's mind to produce thoughts.[3] I believe it is those very thoughts that move us to healthy or unhealthy behavior. I am going to expand this definition to a more applicable use for the purpose of this book. Below are seven perspectives about healthy "thinking" to consider as you read on:

> 1. Thinking is the missing ingredient too often left out of daily life.
>
> 2. The lack of thinking may be the main reason why people fail to achieve their purpose or destiny.
>
> 3. Thinking: The gap between what you want to achieve and your ability to achieve it.
>
> 4. Thinking: Not a vague concept, but a process using your brain that requires the proper analysis of information that results in a decision.
>
> 5. Thinking: A discipline of relating together who you are in Christ, a truthful assessment of your abilities, and making better decisions daily.
>
> 6. Thinking: A required skill in understanding how the world we live in operates vs. how the Kingdom of God operates.
>
> 7. Healthy thinking: A discipline that will renew your mind, thus transforming who you are.

Chapter 1
Thinking...The Missing Ingredient

There is something deep inside calling you. Something in your life is not right, or balanced, or not in the proper priority. You sense there is something you are supposed to be doing, but you are not sure what it is. WHO AM I? The answer to that question lies in your destiny or purpose, and that purpose is so simple, it eludes the greatest of men. **That destiny or purpose is for YOU to be YOU.** I mean the real you, the one that God made. The Creator's master plan goes way beyond the life here on the earth. There are billions of tasks that need to be done on Earth and in Eternity, some of which have your name on them. Paul the Apostle mentions this very point in the book of Ephesians 2:10 - "For we are God's workmanship, created in Christ Jesus to do good works, which God prepared in advance for us to do."[1] The reason you possibly may not be happy or content in your current circumstance is because maybe you are not on the "right" path. God wants you to be you, and that's it! God desires you to be transparent before Him, which requires humility and honesty. Every person on the entire planet has been given four basic areas or tools in order to achieve the YOU. These tools are a set of Skills, Passions, Dreams and Visions or SPDV. The proper development and execution of your SPDV tool set is the 'real' YOU. If you are not moving in the right direction, where do you start? You start by THINKING. What we think about usually determines what we say.

Philippians 4:8

"Finally, brothers, whatever is true, whatever is noble, whatever is right, whatever is pure, whatever is lovely, whatever is admirable –if anything is excellent or praiseworthy – think about such things."[1]

The health of your intellectual, moral, and spiritual state is at risk when you decide to ignore God's nudging of who he made you to be. This action can lead to a level of emptiness in our lives until we come to God and ask him to show us who we are.

One of my favorite movies of all time is the "Wizard of Oz." The character that is most applicable to this book is the scarecrow. His goal was to go see the Wizard, so he could get a brain. As the story went on, he found out that he already had a brain. The problem the scarecrow had was that he undervalued the use of the brain he already had. Once he realized his brain's potential, he developed it by actually using it to solve problems along the way. He was really trying to find himself. So, in essence, I am saying USE YOUR BRAIN!!!

The Thinking Revolution

As you remember this great children's classic, think about your own life and current circumstances. Circumstances are good or bad based on God's perspective, not yours. I say this only with respect to us not being able to predict the future. There have been many times when I thought a circumstance had negative impact on my life, but it was actually a lifesaver and a wakeup call. An example of this can be job experiences. We all have had that job that we really wanted, but it didn't happen. You then find out the company laid off the entire department where you interviewed for the job. That God-led circumstance may have had a negative short-term impact, but a very positive long-term impact. Therefore, be careful how you assess where you are.

Let's assume you have finally decided that you are not thinking as efficiently as possible, so it is time to transform and think more like Christ. The prophet Isaiah agrees with this thinking in Chapter 28:16 - "So this is what the Sovereign LORD says: "See, I lay a stone in Zion, a tested stone, a precious cornerstone for a sure foundation; the one who relies on it will never be stricken with panic."[1] In essence, he is saying Jesus is our foundation. He is the measuring stick for Renewed Thinking. You may not know the way to get to Him exactly, but Jesus says, "Come to me."

The journey to Christ is about to begin, so picture yourself at the edge of a forest. It is called the Forest of Light and Darkness. You have on hiking boots and comfortable clothes that will never wear out. You also have a backpack that contains some items you need, some items you don't need and a list of items to find along the way. The journey will be sometimes pleasant and other times, not so pleasant. Remember to stay on the Lighted path!! Now, off you go to find your destiny.

First and foremost, the foundation for Renewed Thinking *is* the Lord. We must believe that God exists; therefore, believing or having faith that you were created by Him and Him alone is key. Hebrews 11:6 says, "And without faith it is impossible to please God, because anyone who comes to him must believe that he exists and that he rewards those who earnestly seek him."[1] This Scripture alone should bring you joy. God himself will reward you if you seek Him earnestly and diligently. The reward is God's choice, and it is his will to give wisdom to those who ask. In the asking though, you must have the right relationship with God first. He is not a magician or a genie, so first seek a relationship with him and establish yourself as a son or daughter.

God has equipped you! Proverbs 22:6 says, "Train a child in the way he should go, and when he is old he will not turn from it."[1] The key words here are 'THE WAY,' which is simply how God designed you to be and your designated purpose(s). A parent's job is not to steer a child toward a parent's dream but toward the things the child is drawn toward or has passions about. I mean positive things. There are skills and passions just waiting to explode that you will never know about unless

Thinking...The Missing Ingredient

you look for them. That is why it is imperative to expose children to a wide variety of sports, academic subjects, the arts, social issues and of course your faith.

I hope that most of us mature in some way spiritually, and this maturity level includes renewed thinking. We should leave child-like thinking behind and start our adult thinking. Apostle Paul speaks of this in his first letter to the Corinthians. He is really urging the church to change their thinking as to be more effective followers of Christ. 1 Corinthians 13:11 says, "When I was a child, I talked like a child, thought like a child, I reasoned like a child. When I became a man (woman), I put childish ways behind me."[1] So if this were changed to a more adult perspective, it would read: *"Now that I am an adult, I will talk like an adult, think like an adult and reason like an adult. I clearly know that I am not a child any longer and have no choice but to mature or change the way I think."* Paul goes on to further drive the point home that using your brain is not just smart, but required to advance in the Kingdom of God. In 1 Corinthians 14:20, Paul writes "Brothers stop thinking like children. In regard to evil, be infants, but in your thinking be adults."[1] Paul is saying as I paraphrase again, hey brothers and sisters grow up mentally. Don't forget the basics of right and wrong as we have taught the children. In reality, there are many adults – in the marketplace, local churches, and the academic world – who act like children and don't realize it. My point is not meant to be offensive; it is just what I see. Paul is telling you and I to be adults – be who God made you.

This in itself is a major decision to be you. You are making a decision to renew your mind...permanently and continuously. We make thousands and thousands of decisions weekly. Decisions are a result of thinking, and consequences are a result of a decision. As a result, a decision can be viewed as good or bad, depending on the consequence. That consequence can come immediately or sometime in the future. By the way, consequences are not necessarily bad. Nevertheless, there is an inherent mistake in this thinking pattern, if you leave God out of the equation. When you consciously and deliberately make God a part of the thinking process, your decisions produce different results. Consequences of decisions that you may have seen as unfavorable, may actually be favorable in God's eyes. We can all agree that God has a better view of your life span than you do, which gives him far more capability to view or judge the weight of that decision.

Now, let's go a little deeper. The Lord desires all of us to be sensitive to him, which is why the Lord Jesus told his disciples to tarry or wait in Jerusalem three day, until the Holy Spirit came upon them. The reason this is important is because of consistency. Sure the disciples could have moved the Gospel forward without it, but not at the level God required. Jesus wanted the same level of communication he had with the Father to be shared by his disciples. It was about consistent work, thought, decisions and actions. So all I am saying is without the Holy Spirit, we can still make decisions, but WITH the Holy Spirit, we have consistency in quality decision-making. The Holy Spirit is the "real" driver in renewing your mind. Now, it gets better. If you are aligned with God and are working in his *Will*, then He can surely make decisions that might have an adverse effect on our lives turn out to be favorable. This does not mean you will not experience pain. As my spiritual mother, Dr. Helen Delaney, has said on many occasions, "It rains on the just and the unjust." The Bible speaks of this paradigm in Ecclesiastes 8:14-17 which reads,

> "There is something else meaningless that occurs on Earth: the righteous who get what the wicked deserve, and the wicked who get what the righteous deserve. This too, I say, is meaningless. So I commend the enjoyment of life, because there is nothing better for a person under the sun than to eat and drink and be glad. Then joy will accompany them in their toil all the days of the life God has given them under the sun. When I applied my mind to know wisdom and to observe the labor that is done on Earth— people getting no sleep day or night— then I saw all that God has done. No one can comprehend what goes on under the sun. Despite all their efforts to search it out, no one can discover its meaning. Even if the wise claim they know, they cannot really comprehend it."[2]

In other words, do your best to stay connected to the Lord in a love relationship. Love Jesus, listen to the guidance of the Holy Spirit and let God do the rest.

That leads us to another one of the Bible's most foundational Scriptures relating to the order of thinking. It is Matthew 6:33 - "But seek first his kingdom and his righteousness, and all these things will be given to you as well."[1] I really love this Scripture, because it gives direct guidance to what God's priority is regardless of how mature a person is. The Scripture applies to both children and adults. The Lord Jesus said to seek out God first before anything else you do. This means daily, we should seek out God's Kingdom, which is full of guidelines, principles, thinking, agreements, warnings, etc. This Scripture also says to seek out God's righteousness, which is the ultimate gift. Righteousness is the exchange of our sin for Christ's cleanliness. That gift, if received properly is the key to heaven. Renewed thinking begins and ends with God!

The Lord has given me a wonderful model to help you renew your mind. The model will outline each stage of importance to get you to that ultimate goal of a renewed mind. It is called Cobb's Renewing Your Mind Model.

Chapter 2
Cobb's Renewing Your Mind Model

Models have been used for decades to establish consistency and quality of results. One day the Lord brought into my spirit Romans 12:2, which is the first time I really asked the questions: How does a person renew their own mind? What does that process look like?

When I did not find any books specifically on steps to renew your mind, I knew this was my assignment to deliver it. The Lord began to pour revelation daily into my soul as well as Scriptures to back it up. The Apostle Paul gave us some great insight into our thinking in 2 Corinthians 4:4 – "The god of this age has blinded the mind of unbelievers so they can't see the light of the gospel of the glory of Christ."[1] I interpreted this Scripture as truth being blocked from a person's thinking because they were NOT already in a certain frame of mind. This is one of the reasons why the "transforming by the renewing of our minds" might be difficult. How can a person transform their mind while being spiritually blind? The challenge was to develop a model to help those who seek this transformation, learn how to do it successfully regardless of current state.

I created a model to help explain my perspective on transformation. See the model pictured in figure below.

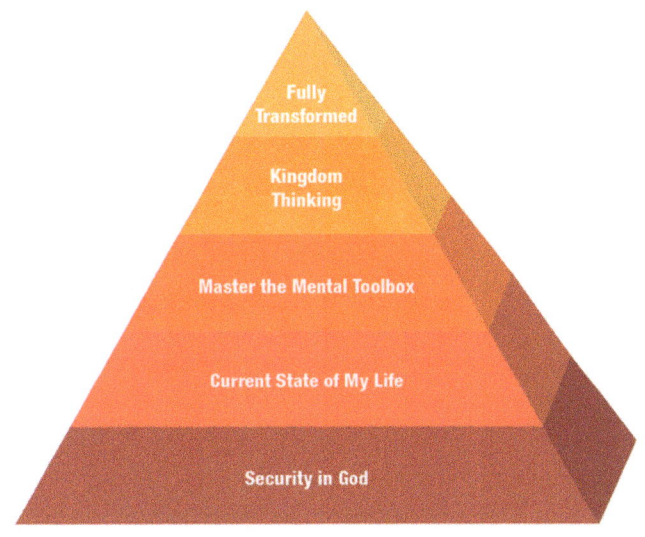

[Cobb's Renewing Your Mind Model]

The Thinking Revolution

This model outlines an approach that leads to personal efficiency by stage. I will discuss each stage briefly, then explain in more detail in later chapters.

Stage 1 is called **Security in God**. Before you can come into full understanding of your destiny or purpose, you first have to gain security in who God made you to be. This means acknowledging that the Lord exists and that he made you for a specific purpose. God wants you to accomplish the dreams and goals that he has placed in you. This stage includes taking inventory of your skills, passions, dreams, and visions (SPDV).

Stage 2 is called **Current State of My Life,** which is how you see your life now.

This is like using a compass to honestly review where you are in life within three major areas. These areas are Faith, Family, and Finances. We are going to walk through some basic questions in each area to help you assess clearly where you are.

Stage 3 is called **Master the Mental Toolbox**. These are concepts like Humility and Gratitude. Once we discuss these, we will outline a simple development plan that you can use to transform by renewing your mind. This plan will include the use of your full SPDV tool set and how to develop it.

Stage 4 is called **Kingdom Thinking**. This is where you become advanced and consistently execute your SPDV tool set and Thinking Toolbox model. You will learn to apply these to life's many scenarios on a daily basis.

Stage 5 is called **Fully Transformed**. You have finally reached this point by much preparation and practice. You have allowed God to change you into a clean vessel for His Glory. This stage is not meant to be perfection, but an ideal state. You will learn to walk in humility and teach others how to transform their lives by the renewing of their minds as well. This will be a continuous process of transforming.

Now, let's look at each stage separately.

Chapter 3
Security in Who God Made Me

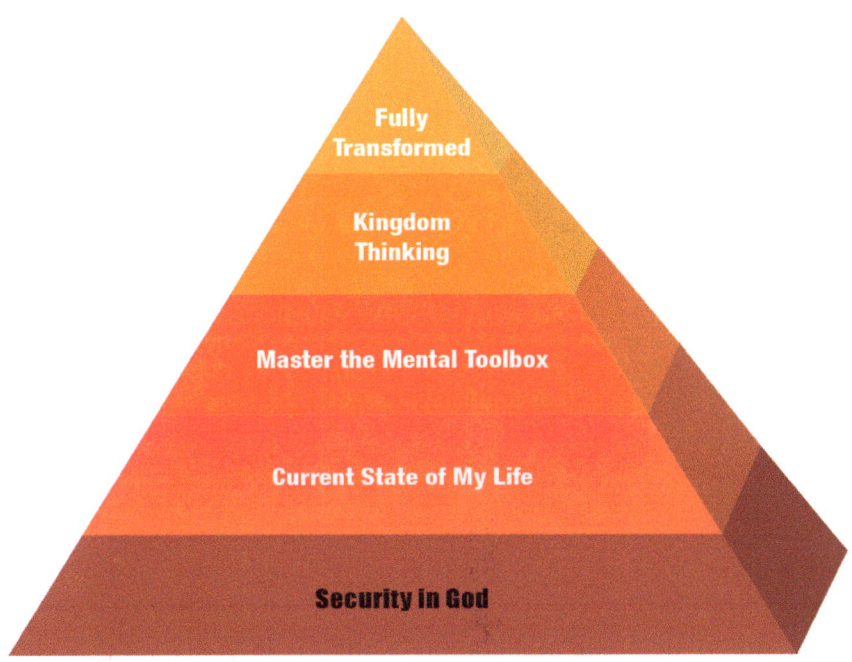

[Cobb's Renewing Your Mind Model]

This stage is about your identity. The goal is to establish who you are and what you are made of. Security is one of the most important aspects of life. We strive to be secure in many areas. Those areas may be in a marriage, friendship, work, volunteering, or church. Most important, being secure in the fact that God made me in His image is an awesome sense of security. If we decide to go there first, all else will begin to come into alignment. There is a reason why God said to seek Him first (Hebrews 11:6). It was for security and foundation.

There is no questioning that God is perfect; therefore, He creates His children for a purpose. Everybody and I mean everybody was and will be created for a purpose, meaning there are no accidents by God. Paul speaks of this in his second letter to the Corinth church. He writes in 2 Corinthians 5:5, "Now it is God who has made us for this very purpose and has given us the Spirit as a deposit, guaranteeing what is to come."[1] The purpose in the case is for everlasting bodies in heaven. This is encouragement to do God's will while on Earth. I learned very early in my life that I could not be anybody else but me. No matter how another person's life might look, it always comes with history and baggage. So goes the saying "the grass is NOT always greener on the other side," meaning trying to be someone else or be in someone else's situation is just a matter of perception not reality. Nevertheless, it was only when I entered my late 30s that I began to actually walk in my purpose. There are things I am still working on to bring clarity and action, like the writing of this book.

If we can agree for now that God made us, then who are we? Can you describe who you are to a total stranger? Can you write down on paper what things make up *you*? When trying to determine the steps of the model, we can break-down the base parts of *you* into four areas: Skills, Passions, Dreams and Visions.

Skills are physical and mental acts that you can do well and that are manifested externally. People can observe and witness these skills. Examples include carpentry, writing, or athletics. Virtually all skills are developed over time by practicing and training. It may take some people 2,000 hours to perfect a skill, but it may take others 10,000 hours to perfect that same skill. It is obvious by viewing basketball, baseball, or football, that athletes display varying degrees of skill in their respective sports. For the most part, those who excel in their physical and intellectual capacity rise to the professional level. A list of some of my skills includes problem-solving, parenting, coaching, and financial analysis. What are some of your skills? Write them down.

Passions are those hidden emotions that arise when certain subjects or causes are present. Some of these causes arouse more joyful emotions while others may evoke negative emotions like anger. Passions can also be for more lustful for material things, so be aware of those. Joyful or negative emotions both channeled in the right manner can bring great success to a career or project. For example, those who have a passion for feeding hungry children will work tirelessly in order to bring food to them. Passions are drivers and sometimes the holders of memories. Think of a time when you really enjoyed something you did. I remember a time after college where I volunteered at senior citizen center to tutor high school kids in math. It was a very rewarding experience, and I enjoyed encouraging and mentoring them along the way. After the tutoring sessions, I went to talk to the senior citizens and played pool. I remember those times and had to ask myself: What fueled that experience? Why did I enjoy it so much? I enjoyed information transfer and encouragement. I was fortunate to get a college degree at the time and wanted to encourage those who sought to understand academics for personal betterment.

Along with that, I enjoyed hearing the experiences our senior citizens were telling me about life. We talked about work, school, community, and politics. I also have had negative experiences that have led to passions. I have always loved basketball and played the sport all the time in my youth, just like millions of kids do every day. I tried out the for the freshman basketball team and did not make it. Well I didn't give up and practiced all school year and all summer. I was coached by my stepfather, who was a semi-pro basketball player. He knew my skills and desire to play

Security in God Who Made Me

ball. I tried again to make the high school sophomore team and was cut on the last list. I was extremely disappointed and felt like I was good enough to be on the team. I still wanted to be a part of the game, so that negative experience drove me to coach instead, which led to teaching and encouraging. A list of some of my passions includes teaching, encouraging, fairness, and business improvement. What are some of your passions? Write them down.

Dreams are very personal. On a higher level they can be a means for God to speak to us. Dreams start from our childhood. Dreams are things you think about where you see yourself in a certain element or environment. There are dreams of all kinds. Some dreams are materialistic, and some dreams are conceptual. Just because you may dream of driving a certain kind of car or living in a nice house does not mean it is bad. Dreams can be fun and full of laughter.

I would recommend a wonderful book about dreams by Bruce Wilkinson called *The Dream Giver*. This is not a technical book about dreams; it is a story about the pursuit of dreams. The way a dream leaves you in the morning may drive you to change course. A repeated dream may be a message from God for you to make yourself available in a different way, like joining a new company or local charity. There are also bad dreams that can be filled with fear, anxiety or sadness. From God's perspective, these dreams may not be "bad," but a warning to one of His children to change behavior or change a given circumstance. These dreams may even be a sign to stop worrying and exercise faith.

I do want to mention that when we have behaviors that are truly ungodly, dreams can turn into fantasies or deceit. If you want a better understanding of dreams, I would encourage you to seek out a trained or licensed professional in this area. Whatever the case, dreams can be useful in helping to lead you in a direction of health, strength, and encouragement. Dreams help you to see into the future. They can give you hope not just for you, but for others as well. The phrase "follow your dreams" is a popular one and those who say it mean it as encouragement. I mentioned earlier that dreams are personal. Others can't tell you exactly why you dreamt a certain dream. They may be able to tell you what the elements of the dream may be like colors, animals, or things, but never the reason. Only God knows, and that is why we must pay attention to them. It is a good idea to journal the dreams that you remember. See if there are any patterns. See if God is trying to steer you in a certain direction. Dreams are a part of who we are.

Lastly, let's not forget the day-dreamers. I am in this group as well. I can see a situation good or bad, and begin to dream about how to fix it, make it better or how to get out of it. The mind is very powerful in creating ideas from a given situation and brain-storming. Again, write these down, and you may enjoy what you see over time. Find someone to share your dreams with, and we will discuss more of this later. A list of some of my dreams includes raising a successful family, running my own business, living debt-free, and accomplishing The Great Commission. What are some of yours? Write them down.

Visions are also a way that the Lord may communicate to you regarding who he has made you to be. He has set you apart from others in the same environment to see how things are suppose to be vs. how they really are. Having vision is having the ability to see things in a certain order or seeing things broadly. I can see a problem and breakdown the individual parts that make up the problem. The next stage is to visualize how the parts relate to each other. I then visualize the solution and put the pieces back in order according to that vision.

Visions are used very frequently in the marketplace, coupled with a Mission. Missions are what you do, but Visions are what you want to become. It is important that the people who work in a same business understand the vision of the company, so they can apply their skills to make it happen. As with dreams, write your visions down. That is exactly what the Lord told the prophet Habakkuk after he complained about the Babylonians. Habakkuk was distraught about how the Babylonians were ruthless and treacherous men who went throughout the region taking whatever they wanted. He was sort of testing God to see what his reply would be. God's response basically told him that he already had the answer. It says in Habakkuk 2:2, "Then the LORD replied: 'Write down the revelation and make it plain on tablets so that a herald may run with it.' "[1] So write down what you see and don't underestimate the power of the written word. As I mentioned before, I wrote this book for only one reason. I saw something going on in our society that the Lord wanted to bring some clarity to. He wanted me to focus on how we think – and more important, how we should transform our thinking. I have seen so many situations where the people were just not thinking right. It wasn't even clear where the basis of the reasoning was coming from. The only way to get this revelation out is to write it down and make it plain. A list of some of my visions includes how to help a company run well, how to run a stable household, and how to properly coach talent in a company for success. What are some of yours? Write them down.

Now that we have discussed the SPDV tool set, take the time to write down who you are in each area. Do this before moving on to the next chapter.

1. **Skills**: Make a list of all the skills you believe you have and then assess them for maturity by placing a 1-10 with 1 being not mature to 10 being very mature. For example:

Security in God Who Made Me

SKILLS	ASSESSMENT
Being A Dad	9
Conflict Resolution	7
Critical Thinking	8
Problem Solving	9

2. **Passions**: Make a list of the passions that you believe drive your behavior. The things that cause emotions and will move you to action.

3. **Dreams**: Write down all the dreams that you remember, even those from your childhood. This may take a little time, but it will be worth it. Also indicate in each dream if you perceive it to be a good or bad dream.

4. **Visions**: What visions do you see? What causes make you think and create visions of order? List these out one by one.

Now that you have done this take a good look at it and start seeing the real YOU. The view that you see in the mirror may be quite different than the one you see on paper.

The Thinking Revolution

Chapter 4:
Realization of the Current State of My Life

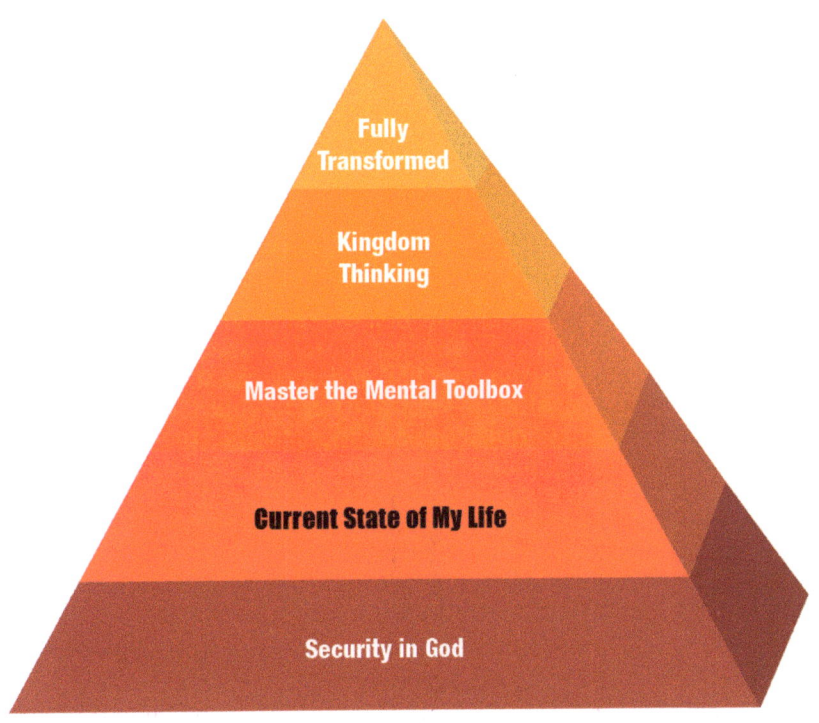

[Cobb's Renewing Your Mind Model]

This second stage is similar to using a mirror and a compass. As you know, a mirror shows your identical reflection. A mirror reflects exactly what it sees without prejudice, politics, emotion, or bribery. You can't ask a mirror not to reflect properly. Once you know what you look like, a compass will come in handy to tell you which direction to go. A compass is an instrument that gives direction. The results of your assessment of your current state will tell you which direction to go in. The main goal here is to know where you are in the areas of Faith, Family, and Finances.

Taking inventory of what path you are really on is very important for thinking about the next steps. It is vital to the model that you have a true understanding of right path vs. wrong path. There are three areas of life that will give you a good barometer or measurement on how well your life is progressing: Your Faith, Family, and Finances. In the church, we talk about bearing fruit. In this we mean the result of deeds good or bad, and how your life affects others. For example, a good deed can be helping someone without them asking, therefore leaving an impression of love. In general, good fruit comes from a behavior pattern of good deeds. The ultimate fruit in God's eyes is presenting Christ to a person that does not know him and behaving in a manner that draws that person to Christ, but not to you. A bad deed may be if I openly criticized or judged a person in front of others, whereby leaving an impression of hate or dislike for another person. If the person I was criticizing discovered the comments I made, the chances of a friendly relationship will decrease. A reduction in friendly relations reduces the chances of influence for the good. Constantly bearing bad fruit will at some point lead you down a wrong path. The discovery that you are on the *wrong* path is the beginning of wisdom. Thinking clearly on how to get on the *right* path to being you is more important.

FAITH

Faith that God exist is the foundation of a healthy thinking pattern, though I know all who read this book may not believe that. When I speak of Faith, I am speaking about what you believe in from a spiritual perspective. What do you really believe? Does God really exists in your life, and, if so, what are you doing to demonstrate that? Are you consistent in your practice of your faith? Are you at peace with what you believe? These questions are important, as they lay the foundation for that right path vs. wrong path conversation. As for me, my faith is continually in exercise mode. My faith is stable, but needs to be exercised daily like a muscle in the body. I am grateful to be given salvation by Jesus whereby exchanging His life for my old one. I have also received the gift of righteousness by the Lord Jesus Christ which I can never earn. Works or deeds can never attain this prize, but good works are still required. I have a loving and working relationship with God through his Son Jesus Christ. I am working daily to be a clean vessel, so God can use my life to help others come to Him.

Before Christ ascended back to heaven, he ordered his believers to go and make disciples of all nations, otherwise known as The Great Commission. For me to contribute to the Great Commission, I have to know who I am in God and who he created me to be. Therefore, Faith in God is vital. I must decrease in all circumstances so that He may increase. I also believe in the Holy Bible, the whole Bible. I believe there is history in the Bible, but would never let it be reduced to a mere history book. God is perfect and thus directed men to write what is written on each page. There is no way in this universe that God would allow men to taint the Holy Bible so that the true character of God is defaced. So I don't buy the argument that man has changed the Bible. The Bible is the undeniable word of God. Reading the Holy Bible is like taking medicine for a sick patient. If you have a sickness that calls for your doctor to prescribe an anti-biotic, your doctor may tell you that "in order for this to work, take ALL the pills for 10 days. Even if it feels like you are getting better, keep taking the medicine until it is gone." So I am here to tell you to take the medicine daily, it is the only way the Lord can create a clear vessel in you. Once you start feeling changed and spirit-filled, keep taking the medicine. The Bible has truly helped me to grow in loving the Lord and humbling myself before him. That is the only way to success and the only way to healthy thinking.

The other important point around solid Faith is sharing it with a group of like believers in the local church. This is a command by the Father to not forsake gathering with the saints. Meaning, you can't grow in faith, humility and love by yourself. There is no way we could be 'good' on our own. Men and women need accountability to become the vessels God desires. I know of only one person who has ever walked this Earth and has accomplished true goodness, and that is Jesus. Bearing good fruit from a practiced pursuit of faith is important. The people who are connected to my life whether they are in the church or the marketplace should be seeing God through me. It is the faith in the Father that must be seen in me, not faith in Myron. I must show the love of Christ daily, so seeds of goodness can be planted in them, so they are encouraged to do the same. Something as simple as a word of encouragement can go a long way. Stopping during your day to speak with someone who is struggling can be a difference in a person making a good or poor decision later. I am not stating this is easy to do daily. We have to invite the Holy Spirit into our lives to be filled daily so that this life is easy and not hard. Dealing with life strictly in the natural only, can bear bad fruit.

FAMILY

Family is one of the toughest concepts on the planet to master. Family can be blood relatives and people who are not blood relatives, but are so close to you that calling them anything else is just wrong. Being a part of a family can be very emotional, so it takes focus and discipline to serve them daily. For me, it took years to take off the clothes of selfishness to become a servant for my immediate family and friends. This is still something that I have to work on daily. If you are married this will be your spouse and children if you have any. If you are single, it may be your parents or a core group of friends who have an open door in your life. Here is the headline: "Your life and those lives around you are connected." They are connected physically and spiritually regardless of your faith.

How you manage your life can positively or negatively affect the people around you. Let's say for example, I don't manage my money very well. I make good money, but spend too much and don't properly account for what I have. A person in the family really needs $50, but because I have not managed my money well, I can't give it to them. I know this may sound simple, but it happens every day. The outcome of the situation connects me and that person. This $50 could have been the gas money for that person to get to a job or doctor's appointment. The proper management of my own finances can bear good fruit in the family or bad fruit. I can bless my family in the areas of money if I am selfless and not selfish. Two major enemies of bearing good fruit in your family are pride and selfishness. Both of these areas will try to isolate you and trick you into thinking the world revolves around you. Well it's not about you, so the sooner you get this concept, the better you will be. Selfishness in particular will lead you to make decisions that appear to benefit you but might not. Recognizing how to be a healthy family member is important. Being stable emotionally and spiritually will help an immediate family stay healthy. Thinking healthy will lead to healthy living. It changes bad behavior into healthy behavior. All of this takes time, studying, and practice.

FINANCES

Money makes the world go around; at least that is what the world says. Everybody needs money at some point to live. Money is a tool that can be misused at any time by anybody. Learning about the traps of money and how to properly use money can never be understated. Money is the root of all evil right? Not quite, the *love* of money is a root of all kinds of evil. Money is mentioned in the Bible 2,350 times. That shows the importance of influence of currency in the world. One of the more influential Scriptures on money is in the book of Proverbs 22:7, which says, "The rich rule over the poor, and the borrower is servant to the lender."[1] The standard in the Bible is to owe no one. People or companies that you owe money can determine your life choices. Therefore, having your finances in order and not living above your means is a sign of the right path. In marriages, the number one cause of divorce is money conflicts, not sex outside the marriage. This fact is very widespread and effects marriages across the board of race and class. Healthy finances can also support charities and ministries.

Chapter 5
Mastering the Mental Toolbox

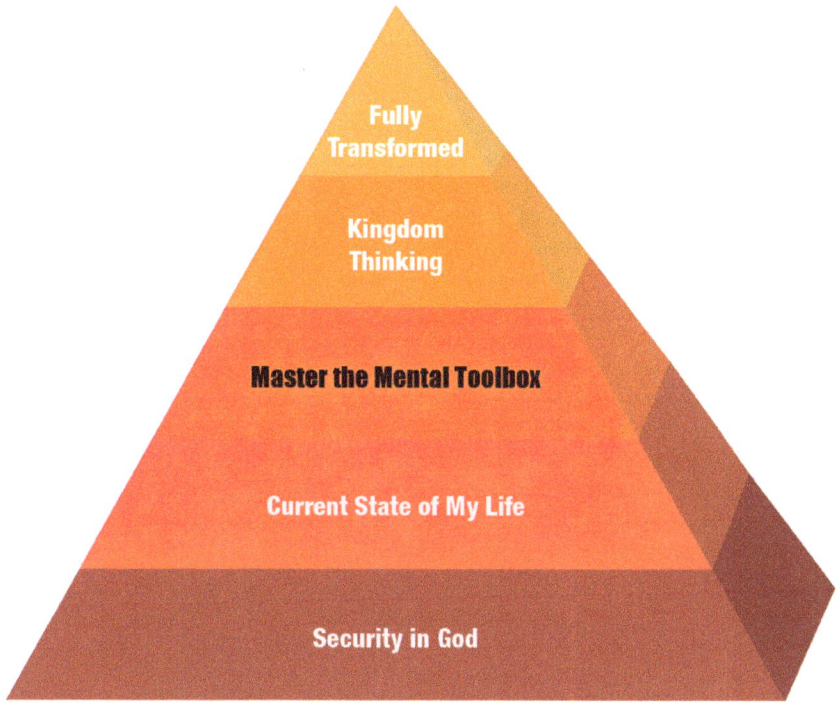

[Cobb's Renewing Your Mind Model]

*Our thoughts are connected to our feelings. Although we cannot change our feelings directly, we can change our thoughts, which in turn, affect feelings. However, it is not always easy to think in a clear, rational, and Christ-like manner. Our thoughts are not always perfect or correct. To develop healthy thinking, we need to acquire and strengthen various abilities. Think of these abilities as tools that help "clear the clutter," that prevent us from making mistakes and seeing things from an incorrect or incomplete perspective. These are not traits or characteristics we are born with. These are skills, like muscles, which strengthen and develop with time.

Dr. Foluso Lawal-Solarin, who is a licensed psychologist, will discuss nine concepts that we have grouped together into our "Mental Toolbox." These are concepts that everyone needs to be aware of and be able to use on a daily or weekly basis to think clearly in most situations. It is our ability to read not only ourselves, but read others that allow us to make "good" decisions. There may be others, but in our judgment, these are the most basic and impactful ones. The list of mental tools are:

1. The Ability to be Grateful
2. The Ability to take Another Person's Perspective
3. The Ability to Forgive
4. The Ability to Delay Gratification
5. The Ability to Take Ownership
6. The Ability to be Organized
7. The Ability to Handle Emotions in an Adaptive Way
8. The Ability to Make, Choose, and Keep the Right Friends
9. The Ability to be Humble

1. The Ability to be Grateful

Research shows that gratitude helps alleviate symptoms of depression. David put on the "garment of praise for the spirit of heaviness." Having gratitude makes you a more pleasant person to get along with. More important, when you are grateful, you have a more accurate perspective on life. People who constantly complain fail to see the "big picture."

How to be more Grateful:

Remember that being more grateful is not being in denial about the difficulty of a situation. We all know of people who can be pretty irritating when it seems like they are trying to ignore the difficult reality of a dire situation. To develop the habit of gratitude, you need to take a more focused and complete perspective of a situation. To build this skill, set aside two weeks, and before going to bed each night, write down three things you are grateful for. Over time, you will begin to see difficult situations from a different perspective. It is not easy at times, and it may take a while for you to see what warrants gratitude. Gratitude can also be likened to being thankful. Being thankful for what you DO have, is one guaranteed action that will keep Satan at bay in your life.

2. The Ability to Take Another Person's Perspective

This ability is similar to empathy. You can take another's perspective without necessarily agreeing with them. This helps you communicate and resolve conflicts more readily. When you take the perspective of someone else, you engage them.

How to take the perspective of someone else:

Take some time after the conflict, when you are alone, to completely immerse yourself in the other person's experience and perspective. Try to see why what the person said may make sense. Pretend that you are his or her lawyer and you are taking up the case. That person may still be wrong, but you have a better view of his or her logical and emotional state by doing this. You have to be careful, because some people will "over identify" and lose objectivity. For instance, if you are a teacher and you have a student who is failing the class, over identifying means feeling so sorry for the student that you change the grade. That helps no one. Taking the student's perspective may mean coming up with a better solution to deal with the low grade. By taking another person's perspective, you become less judgmental, and you are able to "speak the other person's language," when it comes to a conflict.

3. The Ability to Forgive

Forgiveness is a key element in spiritual victory. God commands ALL believers to forgive, because he knows the condition of the heart if not done so. It is so important that it is one of the "deal-breakers" that Jesus mentions in the Bible: He says he will not forgive us if we don't forgive others! Unforgivingness is described as "torment" in the Bible. Psychological studies show that those who forgive are more mentally and physically healthy than those who do not. If you can't forgive, you are going to be held back in so many areas spiritually. Those who don't hold on to offenses are more free to serve others, learn from God, relate to others, and progress, instead of always living in the past. When you forgive, you are more joyful, and you can have the mind of Christ.

Steps on How to Forgive:

The Thinking Revolution

Step 1: Count the Cost. This is a real challenge for some people, including myself. One thing to remember is the sobering message from the Lord in the Bible: If we don't forgive others, He won't forgive us. Is the person that offended you worth losing your eternal salvation and going straight to hell? How effective can you be as a parent, friend, or co-worker if your heart is hardened toward others?

Step 2: Admit what was done, be honest about your feelings, and be honest about the wrong that was done to you. After all, if there was no wrong done, what is there to forgive? Be honest to God first of all, and allow yourself to fully feel the pain. Then ask God to heal you. When we say this, there are just some things that you can't do yourself. If we could do everything ourselves, we would be perfect and not need God. This is not a one-time event, but needs to happen as often as you remember.

Step 3: Ignore everyone else, for a moment. Put everyone else out of the picture. Forgiveness has nothing to do with the person that offended you. There is nothing special about them that deserve your forgiveness. There is nothing "understandable" about the sin that was committed. Don't focus on making allowances or excuses for what was done to you. Sin is sin. Instead, focus on your relationship with the Lord. In the Bible, Jesus shares a lesson about an unforgiving debtor. He owes millions of dollars to a lender, can't pay, and begs for patience with the lender. The lender has pity on him and cancels all of his debts. This same debtor is owed a few dollars by a worker of his, but when he had the chance to forgive the worker's debt, he choked him and threw him into prison, and demanded he remain there until the last few dollars of his debt were paid off. When the lender of the debtor heard about this, he in turn threw the unforgiving debtor in jail to be tortured until the multimillion-dollar debt was paid off. The use of debt in this story translates into unforgivingness. When you do not forgive, you are tormented! The other person is living their life, likely unaware or unsympathetic of what you are going through. Unforgivingness unchecked can lead to hate, bitterness, and spiritual death.

Step 4: Focus on the Word of God, not bad advice from others. Perhaps the worst advice I've heard on forgiveness has come from Christians. Pointless clichés such as "forgive and forget" have no basis in the Word of God. When you find yourself dwelling on past hurts, you cannot make yourself forget. People can block out memories, but as a psychologist, I can tell you firsthand that those memories are never really gone. They will find other ways to manifest themselves and exert undue control over the person's behavior. Other bad advice I have heard involves minimizing what the other person did. "It's not that bad, really! They just didn't know. They didn't mean to hurt you. You're just being too sensitive."

There is no way for you to always know what was in the person's heart who offended you. They may have hurt you intentionally, or it may have been a simple misunderstanding or miscommunication. Depending on their character and how well you know them, you can make an educated guess, or come straight out and ask them, but remember that it is not up to you to decide. That process is not essential in forgiveness. Joseph went through numerous trials. When his brothers asked for his forgiveness, he did not minimize their sin, or make excuses for them. He said, "Am I God that I should punish you?" Then he went on to describe how even though they intended harm for him, God used it for good. Focus on the good that will come out of the evil that was done to you. I can think of instances where people have intended evil for me, whether it was to cause division between me and my husband, or to make themselves look better than me because they were jealous or insecure. Because God gave me the grace to forgive, God has caused an even stronger bond between my husband and I, and I have learned to gain my security from the Lord.

Step 5: Remember what forgiveness is NOT. Forgiveness is not forgetting, not trust, or not reconciliation. We are called to forgive all offenses, not to trust all people and not to be in relationship with all people. Trust needs to be earned; the Proverbs are full of warnings for us to be discerning in our relationships. Sometimes people believe that to forgive someone is to immediately let them back in your life, even though the other person is still not trustworthy, or both of you are not willing to be reconciled to one another. Ask the Lord for wisdom in these areas. Some people in the Bible did actually part ways after reconciliation. Esau and Jacob did, as did Abraham and his nephew Lot.

4. The Ability to Delay Gratification

This mental skill can also be to exhibit self-control or be future oriented. Several studies have shown that this trait has been linked to success in life. A study found that kids who showed this trait in elementary school held better jobs, had fewer problems with drugs and alcohol, and were better adjusted adults. Several chapters in Proverbs talk about this ability, like the ant who works hard and stores for the winter, like the wise virgins, who had oil in their lamps and were allowed into the wedding. By having self-control we are able to slow down the worldly process of "I want more...now." We see too many people making poor decisions because they wanted something now. A person may want a new car now, but end up getting a lemon. Delaying gratification can save people a great deal of heartache and regret.

5. The Ability to Take Ownership

The Bible tells us that we need to assess ourselves "soberly." People in the Bible who were victorious owned their mistakes. When David was confronted with his sin with Bathsheba, he said to God, "Against you have I sinned." No excuses. As a psychologist, I have seen that one key in people overcoming difficulties is "owning their role" in life's difficulties. Those who always play the victim and never assess how they can change or improve are perpetually miserable, always believing that they have no control over life's circumstances. Taking ownership means having healthy boundaries, and focusing your energy and effort on what you are responsible for and what you can change. Taking ownership means not being preoccupied with yourself, but seeing yourself in the "big picture"- what you are responsible for, and what you are not. By taking ownership in situations, you can assess situations more clearly, and make more consistent decisions.

6. The Ability to be Organized

Planning and being mindful of what you need to do is important daily. Do you ever know WHY you do what you do? Do you go from Point A to Point B in life without asking yourself where you are going or how you are going to get there? Are you always reactive, instead of proactive? If you do not execute a focused, purposeful action plan in your everyday actions, you will go nowhere quickly. Being able to execute your life, and be mindful, not absent-minded, in your daily activities, means more success and getting along better with others. The Bible, particularly Proverbs, shows us how important it is to plan. People who plan their lives well have accountability, have a stable support group, and have a "plan B" for when things don't go as expected. They don't anxiously plan, but they foresee potential hazards in life and organize their lives in such a way in which they steer clear of these.

7. The Ability to Handle Emotions in an Adaptive way

Our emotions have various functions. If we ignore them completely, or if we completely succumb to them, our thinking and decision-making are adversely affected. Our emotions are not necessarily good or bad in what we do with them is far more important than judging them. Jesus was moved by compassion and fed thousands of hungry people. He cried when Lazarus died, therefore acknowledging his emotions. However, He was not ruled by them. In the Garden of Gethsemane, He said He was "overwhelmed with sorrow to the point of death." He did not want to go to the cross and asked God to take this dreadful task away. But He did not succumb to his emotions. When we are ruled by emotions, we make poor decisions and our thinking is adversely affected. When we learn to handle them in an adaptive way, they can be powerful sources of information and motivation.

Mastering the Mental Toolbox

Steps on how to handle emotions:

Step 1: Learn to describe the emotion that you are feeling. Discipline yourself to use the actual word. Describing your feeling as "weird" or "bad" is not specific enough. If you have persistent difficulty with this, you may want to talk to an experienced counselor to help you develop emotional awareness.

Step 2: Name your feeling, and don't judge it and cover it. If you are feeling envy, jealousy, arrogance, admit what you feel. You don't have to literally stop an activity to do this, but resist the temptation to file your feeling away or repress it. It will not just go away.

Step 3: What you do with your feeling is most important. Your feeling can serve as an important compass, pointing you to the root of an issue that needs to be dealt with. It can also be a powerful motivator. Fear can point to a lack of safety; envy can signify insecurity; and anger can signify unrealistic expectations or a violation of boundaries. Identify the "target" and deal with it through prayer or counseling.

8. The Ability to Make, Choose, and Keep the Right Friends

How are friends defined? As our culture has become more technological, the definition of friend has become more broad and superficial. People who have multitudes of friends in cyberspace may have little experience with or knowledge of what it means to be a friend in real life. However, when we look at successful people in the Bible, they were surrounded with trustworthy people who fostered and encouraged holiness and a more intimate walk with Jesus. The Bible tells us that "bad company corrupts." You will adopt the habits, mind-sets, attitudes, and lifestyle choices of the people you surround yourself with, whether you like it or not. If you are constantly around those who do not follow the Lord, you will be more like them than you are like Christ, even if you do not copy all of their habits. I recall a time in my life when I had friends, some of them were Christians, but they were not very strong in their faith. I do not believe they were fully submitted to the authority of God in their lives. God put people in my life that were strong Christians, but I never made the effort to befriend them, and I paid the price with distance from the Lord and some poor decisions. The "moral of the story" is that you will take on the traits of those who you are around. I know that some of the best and worst decisions I have made are linked to who I have surrounded myself with.

The Thinking Revolution

Every Christian needs some form of accountability, besides a spouse. Having two or three people that you can confide in, who keep you accountable, and who most of all, point you back to the word of God are more valuable than you realize. If you find yourself squirming as you read this, ask God to help you deal with your pride. It is hard for us to admit that we need others, but we do. Many verses in the Bible talk about how friends help build one another up, and how we learn through serving one another. All of us have had bad experiences with friends at some point or another, but that does not mean we write people off entirely. Jesus was betrayed by Judas and Peter, but He moved on, and so can we. We learn through the mistakes of bad friendships about how to choose (and to be) better friends. It is important to remember that while friendships can be fun, you are looking for encouragement and accountability in your friendships. You want a friend who's keeping their eyes on you, and who also has your back. The Bible says that our hearts are deceitful, and there are some issues that we may be unwilling or unable to see without the help of a friend. The Bible says that wounds from a friend can be trusted, meaning that a friend may tell you a truth that is painful. I have received such wounds, and am a better person for it. You want a friend who will encourage you and keep you accountable, not somebody who is controlling, or who sugarcoats the truth and is afraid of confrontation (Remember the story of "The Emperor's New Clothes"?). Don't focus on exteriors, such as race, age, or occupation. Some people never pursue a potentially valuable friendship with somebody else because they have a different job, are of a different race, age, social, or political background. You may find the best friends in the most unlikely places. Ask God to bring the right friends into your life. You will be amazed at how a prayer as simple as this can open your eyes to what you have been missing.

How to choose and keep the right friends:

Step 1: **In order to increase the quality of your friendships, you need to be intentional.** Make it a point to meet with one new person a month. It does not have to be anything complicated or lengthy. Meet at your local coffee shop or set up a time to talk on the phone. Look for friendships that build up your relationship with Christ.

Step 2: **Take inventory of people you spend your time with.** What are their priorities? Just because somebody is a Christian does not mean you share the same priorities. Many Christians still put earthly things as priorities, such as happiness, a perfect family, or material success. If their priority is not spiritual maturity and making God known, find different friends. Of course, if you are actively witnessing to them, that is another matter. That is called discipleship. But make sure that is the case. Some people use the excuse that since Jesus hung out with sinners, you can too. That's fine, if you have the same purpose Jesus did.

Step 3: **Branch out.** For some people, their only friends are their spouse and family. I can tell you right now that is not very healthy. I have seen people that can never accept an in-law or new member in the family because they feel they have "stolen" their child, sibling, or parent. Many of these people never branched out to develop friendships, relationships, or interests beyond their family. I have seen people very resistant to their spouse growing academically or socially because they are so dependent on them for all their needs. No one person is meant to fulfill all your needs except Jesus Christ. To borrow from "Love and War," by John and Stasi Eldredge, we are all broken people. Another broken person cannot complete you. Furthermore, you will drain and cause resentment to those who you depend on excessively. Your family of origin is full of important people, and it is a place you start out in life, but if you are married, the word of God calls you to leave that family of origin and to create a new spiritual family with a spouse. And even with that spouse, your job is to serve in the body of Christ and bring people to Jesus. Again, no one person is designed to fulfill your needs. That comes from Christ alone.

Step 4: **Avoid people who are too controlling.** Some people expect unconditional compliance in a friendship. They become a parent, telling you what to do. They get mad if you don't do things their way. They give you advice without you asking for their permission. This type of relationship is wrong because we are called to follow God, and submit to our leaders. A friendship is not a leadership, parental, or authority based relationship.

Step 5: **Avoid people who are too passive.** We've all experienced friendships or relationships where it seems like we are doing all the work. The word of God says as "iron sharpens iron, so one man builds up another." Friendships are mutual. Do a study of the friendships in the Bible; no one person does all the work.

Step 6: **Be flexible and move on.** Some friendships, after some time, are not working out. Do not become so attached to one person that you can't hear God's voice when you need to move on. At the same time, don't be so willing to run that you ditch every friend that you feel offended by. Friendships have seasons, some short and some long. Listen to God's voice. He will speak to you.

9. The Ability to be Humble

This is not a meek, self-deprecating, "poor ol' me" approach. It does not mean having a low opinion of yourself. Humility means not thinking of yourself at all, unless it is in the context of how God wants to use you. Pride comes from thinking too much or too little of oneself, placing too much trust in our own abilities or focusing too much on our shortcomings. Humility means we realize that our shortcomings or our strengths are tools in the hands of our Maker, and we are always looking to see how we "fit" into His plan and what "gaps" exist that fit the "shape," which He has created us to be. This concept of humility is very counter-cultural, yet, it is necessary for our salvation and following Christ.

Steps to Humility:

Step 1: **Resist the urge at times to offer your opinion or perspective.** Ask yourself, is this really necessary? Ask more questions in a conversation.

Step 2: **When you find yourself worrying about what others think of you, ask what is more important**, people's opinion or God's assessment of you.

Step 3: **Ditch the "pity party."** When you find yourself thinking too little of yourself, remember that you are placing your opinion of yourself above God's. Putting yourself down does not earn you brownie points with God or others.

Step 4: **Stop comparing yourself to others.** Your only standard is the purpose for which God has called you.

Chapter 6
Kingdom Thinking

The Transformation Development Plan (TDP): How to create one and stick to it

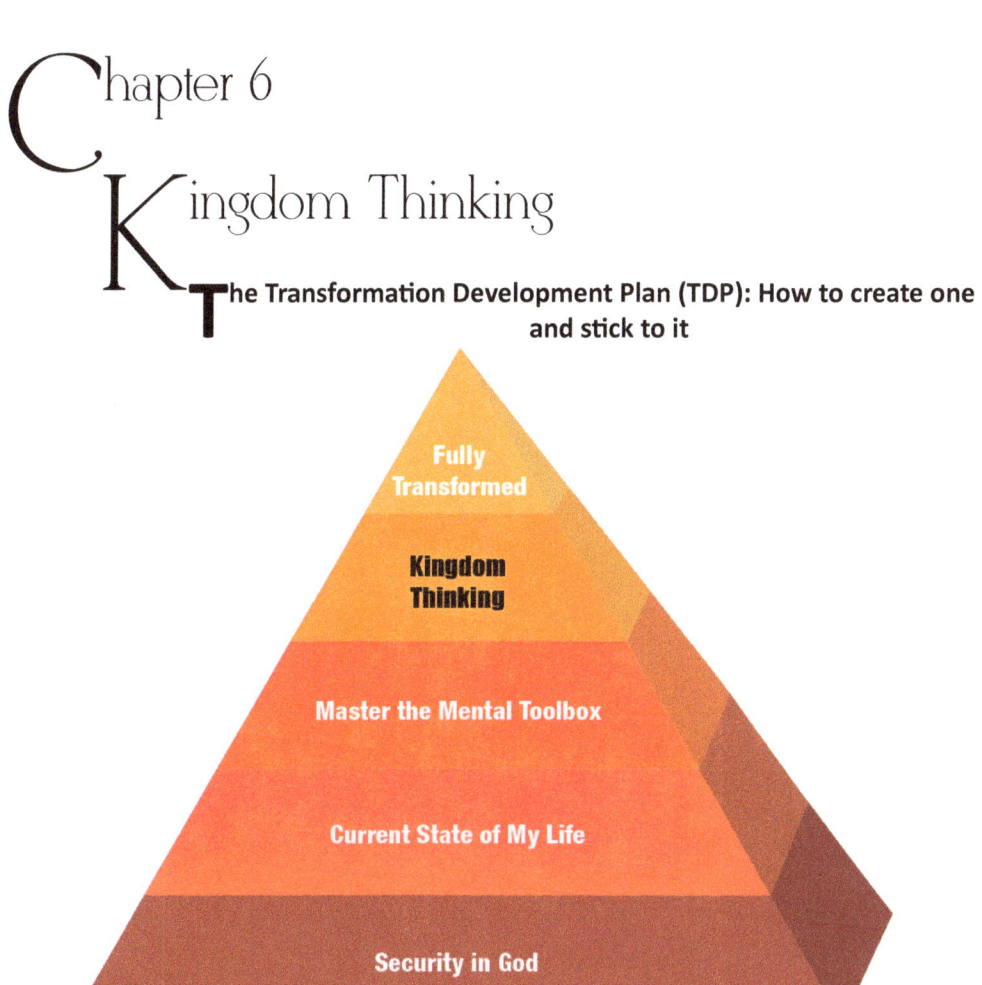

[Cobb's Renewing Your Mind Model]

We will illustrate this TDP by means of a short story. The TDP or journey we are speaking about will transform a person's life by renewing their mind, thus changing their behavior to bear good fruit.

Paul is a new small group leader in a medium-size church in the city of Bella, which is 30 miles north of the great city of Toobusytothink. The name of the church is called Wisdom Church. He co-leads with his wife, Autumn, this group that consists of five families. The makeup of the group is three married couples and two single people. The group is now 2 years old and running well, but it didn't start out that way.

Autumn was already in the local church before marrying Paul and was spiritually more mature than him. Paul had a heart for the Lord's work and was a called to lead a little later in life than Autumn. Paul was an intellectual at heart and by his nature was more earthly minded than Kingdom minded. Two years before they decided to be leaders of a small group, Paul realized he needed to be more Kingdom minded before starting a small group with Autumn. He wanted to leave the patterns and behaviors of the world, but be transformed in the likeness of Christ. Paul wanted to think like Jesus does and therefore had to renew his mind. He went on the journey that everybody has to travel if they want to be transformed. He traveled through the Forest of Rain or Shine. Before going, he started with exercising his Faith that God existed and that he would find what he was looking for. The Lord has always been clear in his commands regarding priorities. Seek the Kingdom of God and his righteousness FIRST, and ALL things will be added. As said earlier in the book, this means Kingdom thinking will be added unto you. Paul knew and believed this. He was very secure in who God made him.

Paul took on his journey proper travel attire so he would be prepared for each day. He put on the following gear:

- A belt that kept his pants up and shirt secure.
- An outdoor vest to keep his chest warm.
- A pair of boots for any kind of weather and terrain.
- A back pack filled with life essentials, such as water, food rations, a journal and a small Bible.
- A snug fitting hat for rain or sun.
- A hunting knife (just in case of predators).

As Paul began his year plus journey, he started to journal the skills he already had that would be needed to lead a successful small group. Some of the skills he already had was facilitating and writing skills. Some weaknesses he needed to improve on was organizing and listening skills. He recognized that he has a real passion for leading others to the Lord, but was not sure if it was a particular passion for youth ministry. He just figured that answer would come with time. He didn't just have one passion, but four, so he noted them all. Also along the journey he began to write about all the dreams he had been having, both good and bad. He wanted to understand them to see if the Lord was speaking to him regarding any areas of his life that needed adjustments or attention – maybe there would be someone along the journey who was skilled in dream interpretation he could ask. Journaling became a weekly learned behavior because without it, how could he keep track of so many areas and questions. Additionally, Paul had visions where he could see the greater good in organizations, processes, and people. He truly believed these visions were from God, but did not know how to order them or where to put them. These Skills, Passions, Dreams, and Visions became clearer as he wrote them down and asked God directly what they were. Over time some questions became clear while others still remained open. Paul took time out weekly to review how God made him.

Kingdom Thinking

He constantly searched his heart for the skills, passions, dreams and visions the Lord blessed him with. In some cases he did not like what he saw. There were some anger issues, impatience and selfishness that he stored up in his heart that could not exist if he wanted to be a successful small group leader.

Once Paul understood these elements of his character, he searched some the major areas of his life like his Faith, Marriage, and Finances. He wanted to be sure that he was performing to the standard Jesus required. This was a little harder to do because of pride and shame. He spoke to his wife about these areas as well as a close family friend his wife knew and respected. Paul's wife has mostly great things to say, but was honest where he fell short in the marriage and some financial areas. Paul and Autumn came into agreement after some tough discussions. They both agreed to put some plans in place to improve weak areas. Paul also used a seasoned mentor to work with him on the skills he didn't have that he wanted to improve. They first worked to make clear the passions God gifted Paul with and how to channel time to develop them. The mentor also suggested ways to connect the dreams and visions to the passions and skills.

One day along the river in the forest, he saw a reflection of his self. This reflection was a revelation on how he interacted with others and saw his own mind-set. He understood the following mental tool models:

- He always had the ability to take another's point of view.
- Make, choose, and keep the right friends.
- The ability to be grateful.
- The ability to forgive.

What Paul realized he had to work on was:

- The ability to take ownership of all his actions.
- The ability to be organized.
- The ability to be humble.

The mental tool models that needed to be attained were included in the TDP. Paul actually had events to attend where it was mandatory to exercise the strong mental tool models and work on the weak ones. Needless to say, this was all not easy and took hard work over a period of two years. There were many spiritual forks in the road. 2 Timothy 2:22 speaks about these forks in the road. The Scripture says "Flee the evil desires of youth, and pursue righteousness, faith, love and peace, along with those who call on the Lord out of a pure heart."[1] So the two choices are clear, you can choose the path of evil desires and immaturity or pursue a Kingdom focused life bearing fruit. The work to improve his thinking still continues. So after those two years of work, Paul was very confident that he could pull his weight with Autumn to have a successful small group at Wisdom Church.

Your Mini Transformation Development Plan

In this next section, we map out five stages that will help you create a mini Development Plan as a live demonstration of how you can transform by renewing your mind. Using the Cobb Renewing Your Mind Model as a guide, you will self-assess and journalize your skills, passions, dreams, and visions (SPDV). Next, you will self-assess your current state of Faith, Family, and Finances. Then, you will review the nine items in the 'Mental Toolbox' and assess your current skill level. In the fourth stage you will put this plan into action and find a coach or mentor to keep you accountable. The final stage calls for putting everything together on a consistent basis. Look for opportunities to help others think differently.

Stage 1: Security in who you are and how God made you.

Step 1: 'Security in God' Agreement.

If you agree that God is your foundation for transformation, sign the below agreement.

I _____ agree that God exists and that He is perfect. God does not make mistakes and made me in the likeness of him. He made me who I am for the purpose of his delight. I am unique and agree to discover who I am as a secure son/daughter of God.

Assessment of your SPDV

Step 2: Skills Assessment

On a scale of 1 – 5, Rate yourself on each of the 10 skills below – 1 being does not have the skill and 5 being you demonstrate this skill consistently.

Skills	Skills Definition	Rating (1 – 5)
Listening	The ability to understand others thoughts	
Written Communication	The ability to communicate via email, letters, or presentations	
Verbal Communication	The ability to communicate clearly your thoughts in most situations to diverse groups	
Conflict Resolution	The ability to understand the root cause of conflict between two people and create agreement and Peace	
Self-awareness	The ability to know what things trigger your actions, inspire you, angers you or motivates you	
Patience	The ability to pause and wait when you are in a rush or want to push others along more quickly	
Self-confidence	The ability to believe in yourself	
Facilitation	The ability to get or coordinate diverse opinions and feedback from a group of people	
Leadership	The ability to develop and communicate a vision or ideas that may inspire others to follow	
Light-hearted	The ability to maintain an inner joy and reflect that attitude on to others	

Once you have completed rating the ten skills, indicate below three of the skills that you rated the lowest. Also list the action you are going to take to improve that skill and when.

Skills	Skills Developmental Action	Due Date

Step 3: Passions List

Write below at least three Passions you feel are embedded in your soul. The pursuits of your passions are directly connected to your energy levels.

_____

_____

_____

Step 4: Dreams List

Write below at least two Dreams that were God inspired. Dreams can be directives or messages from the Lord.

_____

_____

_____

_____

_____

Step 5: Visions List

Write below at least two Visions that were God inspired. Visions are the way you see the big picture in ministry, the marketplace or the Kingdom of God at-large.

_____

_____

_____

_____

_____

Stage 2: Realization of the current state of your life in the areas of Faith, Family, and Finances. Being secure, humble, and honest about where you are in life.

Step 6: Current State Assessment

On a scale of 1 – 5, Rate yourself on each of the three major areas of your life. 1 being I am not performing well in this state and 5 being you consistently perform well in this state bearing fruit.

Current State Area	Current State Definition	Rating (1 – 5)
Faith	Do you have personal relationship with Jesus Christ? If so, are you bearing fruit for Kingdom, sharing the faith with others?	
Family	Is there peace in your home? Are the relationships directly around you healthy and have clear boundaries? Do you have goals?	
Finances	Are your finances in order? Do you have gainful employment or skills to attain gainful employment? Have you taken classes on money management?	

Once you have completed rating the three Current State areas, list the actions you are going to take to improve that area and when.

Finances		

Stage 3: Fully developed mental tool model. Mastering the 'Mental Toolbox'

Step 7: Mental Toolbox Assessment

On a scale of 1 – 5, Rate yourself on each of the 9 mental tools below. 1 being does not have the mental tool and 5 being you demonstrate this mental tool consistently.

Mental Tool	Mental Tool Definition	Rating (1 – 5)
Gratefulness	The ability to be grateful for what God has given you	
Empathy	The ability to take another person's perspective	
Forgiveness	The ability to forgive	
Delayed Gratification	The ability to delay gratification. Being patient	
Taking Ownership	The ability to take ownership of our own actions	
Organizing	The ability to organize, plan, and be mindful of time and space	
Emotion Management	The ability to handle emotions in an adaptive way	
Friendship Selection	The ability to be make, choose, and keep the right friends	
Humility	The ability to humble yourself	

Once you have completed rating the nine mental tools, indicate below three of the mental tools that you rated the lowest. Also list the action you are going to take to improve that skill and when.

Mental Tool	Mental Tool Developmental Action	Due Date

Stage 4: Kingdom Thinking and consistent application of my SPDV and mental toolbox models to everyday situations

Step 8: Action the Transformation Development Plan

This is the stage where you begin to think differently, thus changing behavior that will bear more fruit for the Kingdom of God. Lay out the following items to get ready for action and coaching:

1. The Skills developmental action plan
2. The list of God given Passions
3. The list of Dreams
4. The list of Visions
5. The Current State developmental action plan
6. The Mental Toolbox developmental action plan

Review these for a day or two before taking any action. Once you are clear these are the items to move forward, search for a suitable mentor, coach or mature, accountable person to share your plan with. Look for social opportunities to increase in weak areas as well as opportunities to demonstrate strong areas. Keep a journal of everything you do so progress or non-progress is seen on paper.

Stage 5: Full transformation of who you are by a renewed mind. You are a thinking doorkeeper and recognized by your social circles as a Kingdom Thinker

Step 9: Ongoing process of being transformed by a renewed mind.

This is a process that will take continuous improvement. Your Transformation development plan should be updated twice a year and reviewed by your coach twice a year. Stage 5 will provide confidence that you are on the right track and hearing the Lord more consistently.

Chapter 7
Fully Transformed Self from a Renewed Mind

(How to maintain transformation by a renewed Mind)

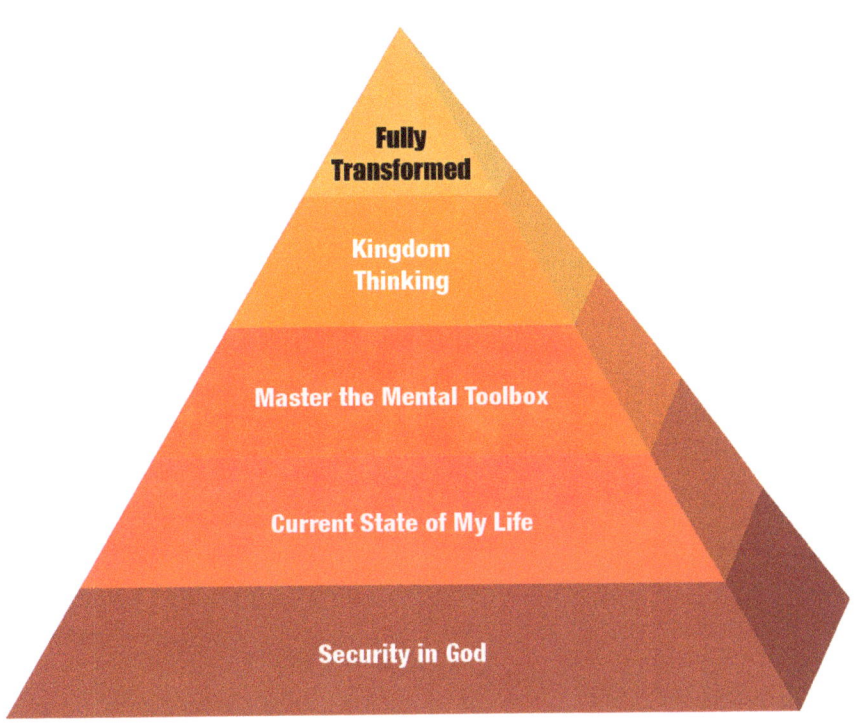

[Cobb's Renewing Your Mind Model]

Romans 12:2

"Do not conform any longer to the patterns of this world, but be transformed by the renewing of your mind. Then you will be able to test and approve what God's will is – his good, pleasing and perfect will."

The essence of this book is to learn how to live a fruitful life. In order to do that, you have to have an inner drive as to why. As discussed in the book earlier, a personal relationship with the Father is vital. Love and oneness with

The Thinking Revolution

God is required to 'truly' transform. It is the *relationship* the Father desires most with his children. Further, heaven is not the prize, God is and his son Jesus Christ. We want to be self-less and used as a clean vessels so God can do his work through us as we live for him.

Transforming yourself by renewing your mind can't be done by you alone. This is accomplished with the help of the Holy Spirit in you. The Holy Spirit has a direct line of communication to the Father so your steps are guided each day. In order to receive those guided steps, you have to be able to think clearly, thus the term Kingdom-minded or Kingdom Thinking. Being Kingdom-minded allows you to be able to truly understand in Faith what God's will is. The approving part of the Father's will is the witness. The will of the Father is made up of three areas:

1. He desires us to grow closer to Him daily

2. He desires all people to be saved and made into disciples of Jesus Christ

3. He desires the greater church to grow spiritually every day. (not just the local church)

One of the Bibles I use is the Life Application Study Bible by Zondervan (NIV)[1]. This Bible includes interpretations to help a user understand Scripture in order to better understand the Lord's heart and the context in which the Scripture is written. The interpretation of Romans 12:2 is so clear, that I could not give it justice by paraphrasing it. It reads:

> "God has good, pleasing, and perfect plans for his children. He wants us to be transformed people with renewed minds, living to honor and obey him. Because he wants only what is best for us, and because he gave his Son to make our new lives possible, we should joyfully give ourselves as living sacrifices for his service."

Christians are called to "not conform any longer to the pattern of the world," with its behavior and customs that are usually selfish and often corrupting. Many Christians wisely decide that much worldly behavior is off limits for them. Our refusal to conform to this world's values, however, must go even deeper than the level of behavior and customs – it must be firmly planted in our minds – "be transformed by the renewing of your mind." It is possible

Fully Transformed From A Self-Renewed Mind

to avoid most worldly customs and still be proud, covetous, selfish, stubborn and arrogant. Only when the Holy Spirit renews, re-educates, and redirect our minds are we truly transformed.1

Once we understand the will of the Father, our thoughts, prayers, and behaviors will fall in line. We will begin to have a mind-set of service with those around us. The more Kingdom-minded people you have in your circle of influence, the more work will get done according to the will of the Father. Jesus spoke numerous times in the New Testament that the Kingdom of Heaven was near. He meant in the hearts *and* minds of all believers!! Deciding to allow the Holy Spirit to renew your mind so you can be transformed in the likeness of Christ is a life-long journey. Preparing yourself daily by putting on the helmet of salvation is key to being focused and clear-minded. Being present-minded in all situations allows the Lord to use you on a moment's notice. At the end of each day, there is a question that should come up in the minds of the Lord's children: Did I miss any ministry opportunities? If the answer is yes, what were you thinking at the time or not thinking? If the answer is no, thank the Lord for an opportunity to advance the kingdom.

Now practically, you have to maintain a working Transformation Development Plan. Review your plan weekly and be persistent to learn what you do not know and to strengthen what you already know. Assess your surroundings and those who are in your areas of influence or circles. Circles of influence may be friends, work, church, community, business, college classmates, etc. Seek to be a doorkeeper for transformed lives by being an example of an active thinker in Christ. We have enough passive people sitting on the sidelines thinking that there is no war to fight. We are not only at war, but are in a raging war for souls, hearts and minds. For example, there is a particular battle regarding the youth in the United States. There is a culture of music, clothes and behavior, that has derailed the thinking of many youth in the country. Many have fallen into the trap of "it is all about me." They feel whatever I don't have, I will get by any means necessary. My point is that you will have to get to their minds before you can get to their hearts. If youth begin to understand their true value and worth, we can begin to shift mind-sets and move toward thinking with clarity. This is only one portion of society and not the only part that needs a new way to think. So, I am appealing to those who have achieved a level of transformation to show the way to those who may need help. Thinking is not necessarily about born intelligence, it is a skill that can be learned by the vast majority of people no matter the age.

Chapter 8
Concluding Thoughts

As you've read through this book, we hope you begun to feel a genuine sense of empowerment. Although books on how to have good marriages, or be good parents are helpful, the degree of success, depends in part, on another person. You cannot change a stubborn child or a self-centered spouse. You can, however, change your own thoughts, behaviors, and actions in any situation. The way you think may not directly change another person, but it can determine how you navigate the most stressful of life circumstances.

As you start to make these changes in your life, remember that it will not be easy. Your friendships, lifestyle, habits, ways of communicating, and some deep-seated beliefs will certainly change. This book may be an easy read, but it can be a challenge to put these concepts into practice. Working these principles out with people you are in relationship with is a great way to move the process forward. Perhaps you may need to work this out in an atmosphere of professional counseling. Perhaps you need to get back to the church and surround yourself with supportive people that can see you through this process. Regardless of the route you take, remember that this is a journey, a step-by-step process. Transformation is continuous as stated clearly in 2 Peter 1:5-8, which reads: "For this very reason, make every effort to add to your faith goodness; and to goodness, knowledge; and to knowledge, self-control; and to self-control, perseverance; and to perseverance, godliness; and to godliness, brotherly kindness; and to brotherly kindness, love. For if you possess these qualities in increasing measure, they will keep you from being ineffective and unproductive in your knowledge of our Lord Jesus Christ."[1] The key words are increasing measure. Once you have the qualities of a transformed life, increase them.

The bottom line as I see it is this: If you didn't make yourself, then God did. Be happy about that. You were designed to do the will of the Father in Heaven. You have deep inside you a dream and a vision to accomplish that in which you were made. You have to outlast the world's culture and be a little bit more focused than yesterday. Discover and improve the skills and passions inside.

The Thinking Revolution

Be disciplined each day and dare to do the impossible through a relationship with Christ. BE TRANSFORMED BY THE RENEWING OF YOUR MIND!! Be a part of the Thinking Revolution. Be Blessed!!

NOTES

NOTES

NOTES

NOTES

NOTES

NOTES

Bibliography

1. Zondervan. The Holy Bible: *Life Application Study Bible (NIV).* Tyndale House Publishers, 1991

2. The Bible Gateway – www.biblegateway.com, March 2012_

3. http://www.merriam-webster.com, January 2012

www.ingramcontent.com/pod-product-compliance
Lightning Source LLC
Chambersburg PA
CBHW062104290426
44110CB00022B/2714